Fencing

By
Maxwell R. Garret

ATHLETIC INSTITUTE SERIES

STERLING PUBLISHING CO., Inc.   New York

The photographic material in this book has been totally reproduced from The Athletic Institute's sound, color slide-film, "Beginning Fencing." This book and the slidefilm are part of a program designed to bring the many benefits of sports, physical education and recreation to everyone through the medium of visual aids.

The Athletic Institute is a non-profit organization devoted to the advancement of sports, physical education and recreation throughout the United States. It functions solely to bring the true values of participation in sports to everyone.

CONTENTS

INTRODUCTION –
FUNDAMENTALS OF FOIL FENCING

Although fencing started centuries ago as practice in swordsmanship for actual combat, it has become identified with the history of man's civilization. Its contribution to society is truly immeasurable.

Today because of the development of light and manageable weapons, many people recognize foil fencing as one of the safest and finest sports for conditioning mind and body. It develops coordination, balance, agility, quick perception, a keen sense of timing and physical endurance for both men and women, young or old.

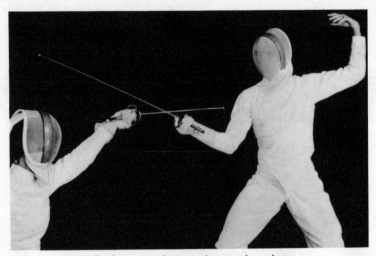

To face an adversary in armed combat
is one of the most exciting experiences
in life. Besides requiring physical endurance . . .

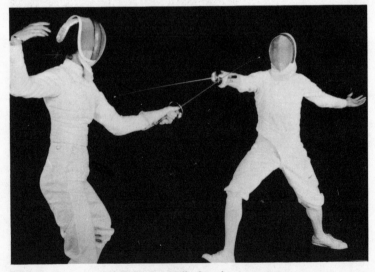

. . . foil fencing calls for clever strategy
as well as lightning swift decisions, for
one must always meet the rapidly changing strategies of an opponent.

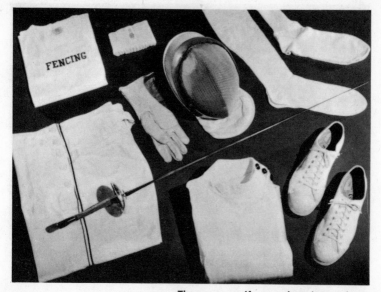

The proper uniform and equipment is essential in preparing to fence—mask, glove, proper shoes, fencing jacket and fencing trousers, undergarments and a foil meeting all standard and *safety* requirements.

Each foil weighs approximately fourteen ounces and has an approximate overall measurement of 42 inches. The blade is rectangular in cross-section and tapers to a theoretical point.

BLADE

POMMEL

BELL OR GUARD

HANDLE

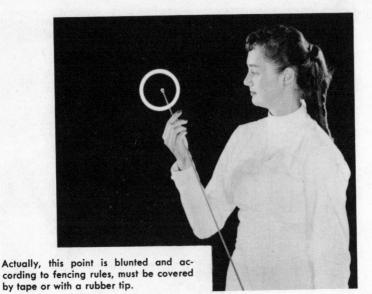

Actually, this point is blunted and according to fencing rules, must be covered by tape or with a rubber tip.

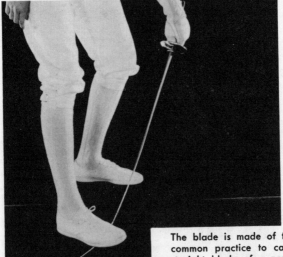

The blade is made of flexible steel. It's common practice to carefully bend the straight blade of a new foil by sliding the sole of your foot along it . . .

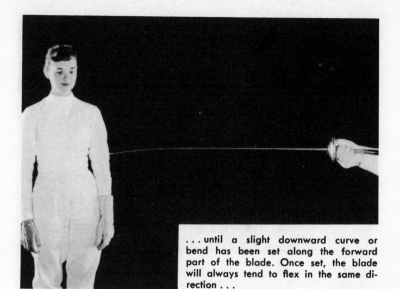

... until a slight downward curve or bend has been set along the forward part of the blade. Once set, the blade will always tend to flex in the same direction ...

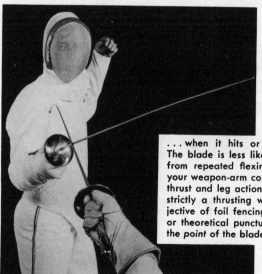

... when it hits or touches the target. The blade is less likely to snap or break from repeated flexing when you extend your weapon-arm correctly and time your thrust and leg action properly. The foil is strictly a thrusting weapon, and the objective of foil fencing is to score touches or theoretical puncture-type wounds with the *point* of the blade only.

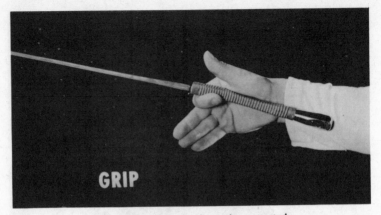

GRIP

The proper grip is best demonstrated
with bell and glove removed. Here, the
handle is correctly held in the palm of
the hand. The forefinger is hooked
around the handle.

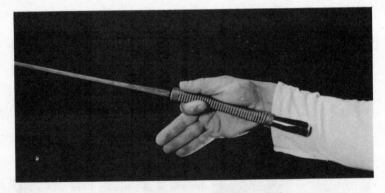

The thumb is now placed on the
handle. (The thumb and forefinger are
called the manipulators.) These two fingers are primarily responsible for the
fine, small movements of the point of the
weapon, forming the basis of finger play.
The action of the manipulators, together
with the rotation brought about by the
ball of the thumb gives the blade the required semicircular or circular motion.

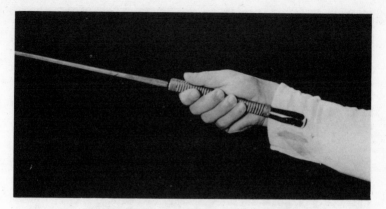

The *other* fingers are now in position on the handle. A fencer's speed of swordplay, point accuracy, firmness and authority in the execution and delivery of his blade, depend primarily on his fingerplay ability.

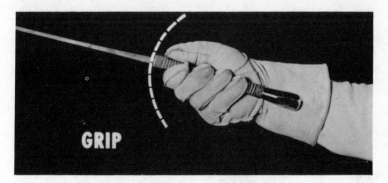

GRIP

Here is the proper grip, wearing the *fencing glove*. The important points to emphasize are: First, *carry the weapon, don't choke it*. Second, hold the foil about an inch from the bell, so the thumb and forefinger do not touch the *inside* of the guard. Third, the thumb should lie flat along the handle and touch the base of the forefinger.

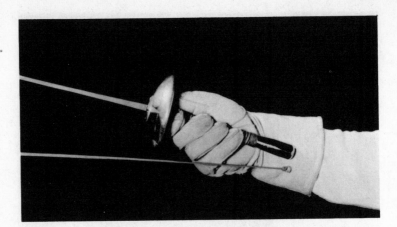

While part of the bellguard's function is to protect the hand, a fencing glove is a necessary safety precaution. Wear it to protect you from the corner edges of your opponent's blade and to prevent the point of his weapon from sliding up the sleeve of your fencing jacket.

The fencing jacket should always be worn during practice and competition. Its snug fit offers aesthetic and practical advantages. In addition, its strong fabric protects your body from injury.

FENCE
SAFELY

Fence safely! Never, under any circumstances, engage in any form of swordplay unless properly protected. Without the mask, even simple practice exercises can be extremely dangerous.

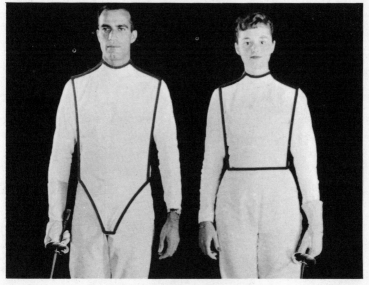

The rules in foil fencing for men and women limit the valid target area to the torso, as outlined.

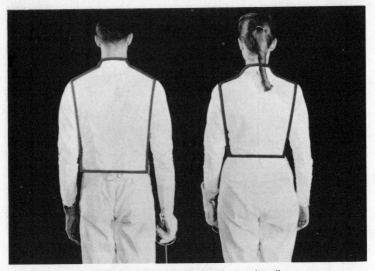

Valid hits can also be made on the rib
cage and on the back.

Touches on the leg and on the mask,
which are outside valid areas, are con-
sidered off-target hits.

The arm and the leg also represent off-target hits. While these hits carry no penalty in formal competition, they stop the sequence of play. The officials call a halt and play is resumed in accordance with the ground rules.

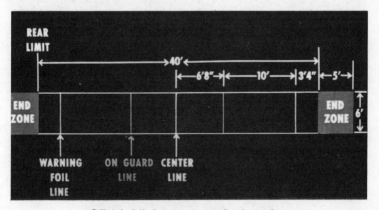

REAR LIMIT

40'

6'8"

10'

3'4"

5'

END ZONE

END ZONE

6'

WARNING FOIL LINE

ON GUARD LINE

CENTER LINE

Official foil fencing is confined to the area of a strip or mat, six feet wide and forty feet long. There is a safety zone of at least five feet in length at each end. While on the mat, fencers are allowed to displace the target, sidestep, turn or half-turn, but must not reverse position.

(Above) Men's bouts are usually fought until one fencer has been hit five times, while in women's bouts until one fencer has been hit four times. The fencer who has been hit the least number of times is declared the winner.

(Opposite page, above) Traditionally, the opponents salute each other before crossing blades. If there are officials and an audience, the fencers salute them, too. Even this salute should be executed in the proper manner.

(Opposite page, below) Standing at attention, with your feet at a ninety-degree angle, salute your opponent by moving your weapon gracefully and smoothly from position one, up to position two, and extended to position three.

THE
SALUTE

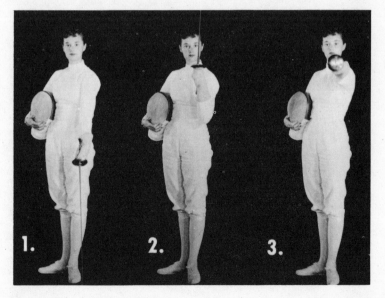

1. 2. 3.

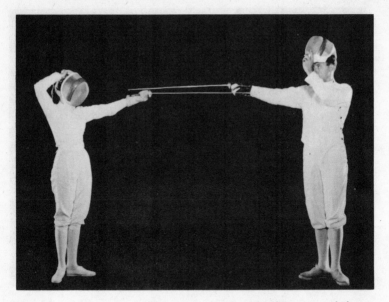

(Above) Now that the formalities are ended, put your mask on, making sure that your chin is resting firmly on the chin pad inside the mask.

(Opposite page, above) You now assume the position of "on-guard." It is the basic position of feet, body and arms which assures proper balance and mobility.

(Opposite page, below) From the on-guard stance you are prepared to execute defensive actions when attacked and to launch an offensive action whenever an opportunity presents itself.

ON
GUARD

ON
GUARD

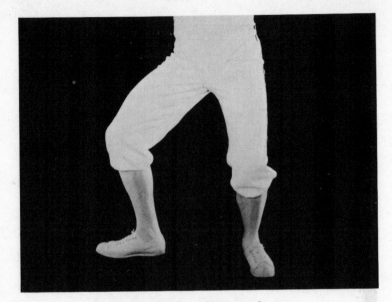

In the "on-guard" position, your feet are
approximately fifteen inches apart and at
right angles. Heels are on the same line.
The leading foot is pointing toward your
adversary, while the trailing foot is
turned at a ninety-degree angle. To as-
sure balance, measure your stance carefully so you carry the weight of your
body equally on both legs.

Then raise your trailing arm and bring it to a position where your upper arm is level with the trailing shoulder, while the forearm forms a ninety-degree angle. Bend the wrist, keeping the hand open, fingers together and point the fingers toward your opponent. Now raise your foil until your hand is level with your breast. When your arm is half-extended, the elbow will be clear of the body and the weapon a continuation of the forearm.

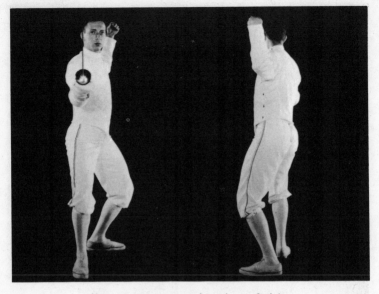

You are now on-guard, and you find it very uncomfortable in the beginning, because the required flexed leg position must carry the weight of your body. However, with practice you will find this stance quite comfortable. Like the cobra, you are in a relaxed position, being able to move from absolute immobility to top speed with power and precision.

Gentlemen, On Guard! With this com-
mand, both fencers cross blades and step
back out of attacking distance.

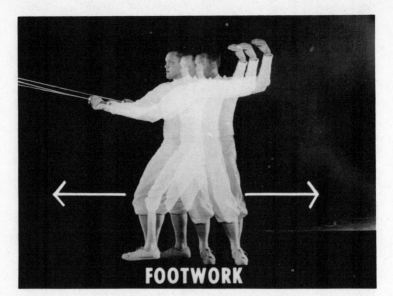

FOOTWORK

Since mobility is an essential of fencing, foot work requires careful study and analysis. Footwork is the action of stepping forward or backward and is used in fencing to gain or maintain distance with your opponent, or to step out of his reach.

ADVANCE

To *advance* is to carry the leading foot
forward first, approximately a foot's
length, and to *follow it up* with an equal
displacement of the trailing foot.

RETREAT

To *retreat* is to carry the trailing foot back first, approximately a foot's distance, and to follow it up with an equal displacement of the leading foot.

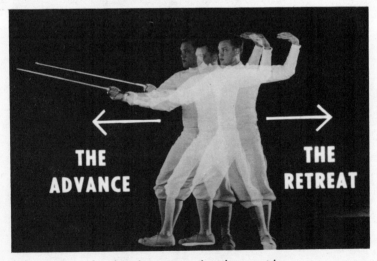

THE ADVANCE

THE RETREAT

In advancing or retreating, there must be no sliding of the feet, no raising of the body. If correctly executed, an advance or retreat will end in a perfect on-guard position.

While practicing footwork, don't drift to the left or to the right, or bob or weave. From the hips upward, the body position does not change. As you step forward or backward, keep at a safe distance from your opponent. A miscalculation of distance can give your opponent an opportunity to score.

Once you have the proper uniform and equipment and have learned these basic positions and moves, you have laid the groundwork for becoming a proficient fencer.

2

ELEMENTARY OFFENSE

With a foil in your hand, it is not too difficult to imagine that you are back in the days of D'Artagnan.

But the modern-day fencer is a far cry from the swashbuckler of old. Modern fencing is a scientific sport that demands self-discipline, control, timing, finesse, conditioning, and practice.

The most exciting phase of fencing is the attack or offense. It may be a lunge . . .

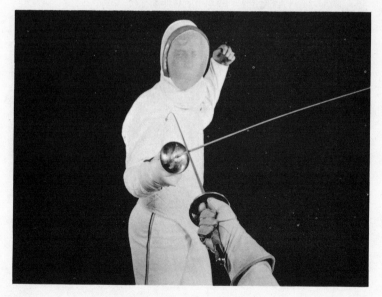

. . . or merely a thrust!

To deliver the thrust, the fencer should
be in the on-guard position, then . . .

THRUST

... thrust! In the thrust, the weapon hand should be extended quickly and smoothly to a position slightly higher than the shoulder, which should not be lifted or contracted. The foil, held lightly, is directed toward the opponent's target, thus identifying the attacker. Through practice you will develop the speed, accuracy and coordination needed to hit your opponent with this *aggressive* action. But, if the target cannot be reached by merely extending the arm, the fencer . . .

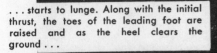

. . . starts to lunge. Along with the initial
thrust, the toes of the leading foot are
raised and as the heel clears the
ground . . .

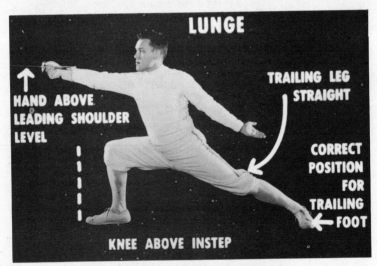

LUNGE

HAND ABOVE
LEADING SHOULDER
LEVEL

TRAILING LEG
STRAIGHT

CORRECT
POSITION
FOR
TRAILING
FOOT

KNEE ABOVE INSTEP

. . . the trailing leg is extended forcefully
to gain maximum drive. The leading foot
lands heel first, while the trailing foot
maintains its original flat-footed position
on the floor.

As the fencer completes the lunge, the trailing arm is extended vigorously behind, ending approximately parallel to the trailing leg. This will help stop the forward body drive in accordance with Newton's law of motion which states "that for every forward action there must be an equal and opposite reaction." This trailing arm extension also helps to maintain balance and limits the target area.

During and upon completion of the lunge, the hips lower with the body, but the head and trunk remain erect with the shoulders parallel to the floor.

Let us try a lunge from the on-guard position . . .

. . . experiencing the feelings of increasing speed and power. . .

. . . moving with perfect balance and coordination . . .

. . . attacking with precision and confi-
dence . . .

. . . to the final hit! The lunge is the most
important offensive movement in fencing
and requires and deserves careful study
and analysis. Since this position is dangerous and tiring, recover immediately.
To recover, the process of the lunge
must be reversed with certain modifica-
tions.

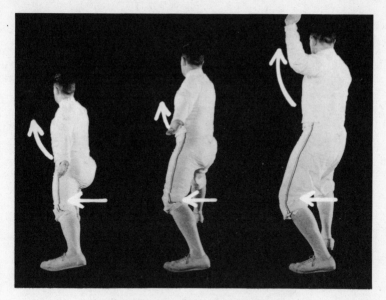

In the recovery from the lunge, the
fencer coordinates the flexing of the trailing leg with the withdrawing movement
of the leading foot and the raising of
the trailing arm.

(Above) To execute the recovery the trailing leg is flexed while the toes of the leading foot are being raised, and by pushing, the heel of the leading foot is cleared off the ground and brought back to its original on-guard position. As this is being accomplished, the trailing arm is brought back to its original on-guard position. The weapon-arm, which has been extended for the lunge, is also returned to its flexed on-guard position.

(Opposite page, above) The recovery must be executed with spring and litheness and perfect coordination. The entire weight of the body is shifted to the trailing leg for a moment during the recovery.

(Opposite page, below) However, there is still another way to recover from the lunge, and that is by recovering forward—pressing the attack!

When recovering forward, flex the trailing leg, pick it up and bring it forward to the on-guard position. Here practically the entire weight of the body is momentarily shifted to the leading foot. During the process the trailing arm resumes its normal on-guard position. The weapon-arm has the option of resuming its flexed "on-guard" position or continuing to press the attack . . .

. . . with another lunge. This movement is
known as a reprise or a re-taking of the
attack.

Whether the return to the on-guard position is made forward or backward will
depend on whether the opponent re-
treats or not.

Since here, the fencer on the right is retreating from the attack . . .

. . . the fencer on the left has recovered
forward . . .

. . . and gained the distance needed to score with the reprise or renewal of the attack.

SIMPLE ATTACK

If an adversary is close enough, a score can be made by a simple attack such as a thrust. But if the fencers are too far apart to reach each other by a simple extension of the weapon-arm, then the extension is followed . . .

SIMPLE ATTACK

... by the lunge. This, too, is a simple attack.

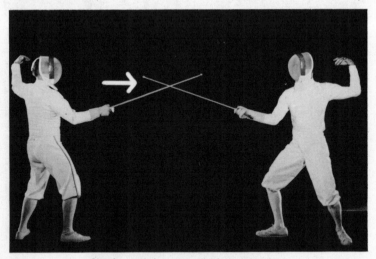

Simple attacks are divided into two
categories, direct and indirect. A simple
direct attack is a single action or movement to the defender's area which is
open to a direct thrust.

SIMPLE DIRECT ATTACK

Here, the fencer on the left has executed a simple direct attack hitting his opponent's target.

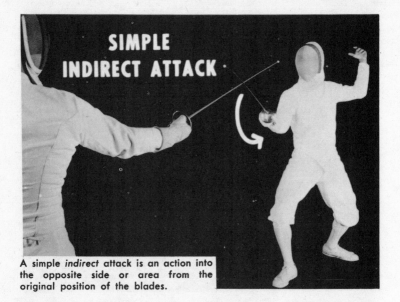

A simple *indirect* attack is an action into the opposite side or area from the original position of the blades.

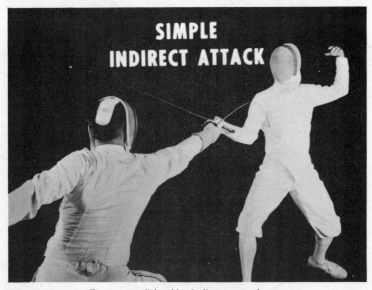

To accomplish this indirect attack requires learning the disengagement.

DISENGAGE

The disengagement consists of dropping the point of the blade, designated by the ball, from the engaged side of the blade . . .

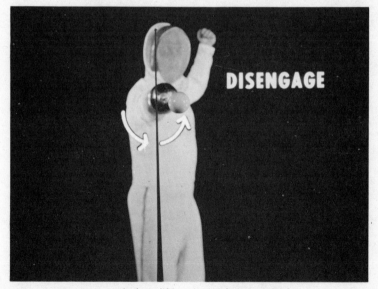

DISENGAGE

. . . and then lifting it to the opposite side with a thrust.

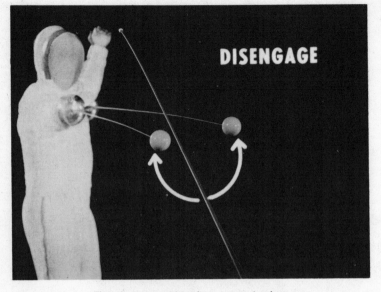

DISENGAGE

The disengage may be executed when blades are engaged or not, with the arm flexed or extended, or a combination of arm and blade movement. The disengagement, more commonly referred to as the disengage, can be done from one side of the blade to the other.

By manipulating the foil with the thumb and forefinger, the point of the weapon is lowered, made to pass under the opposing blade . . .

. . . and raised again in line with the opponent's target while executing a threatening movement of the arm extension. The passing of the point and arm extension are combined with the lunge for the simple *indirect* attack. Like the straight thrust and lunge, the disengagement and lunge become *one* flowing movement. So far the attacks have concentrated on the high target areas.

But simple attacks can also be effectively
executed into the low target areas.

Engaging blades high, a fencer should
have no special difficulty directing a
simple disengage attack towards the low
target area . . .

. . . and scoring!

Engaging blades low, a fencer should
have no special difficulty directing a
simple disengage attack towards the high
target area . . .

. . . and scoring!

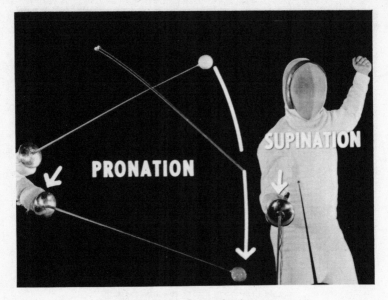

PRONATION

SUPINATION

In executing attacks to the low areas, whether the hand should finish in pronation (fingers and palm at 6 o'clock position) or in supination (fingers and palm at 12 o'clock position) is dependent upon the fencer. The object of the attacking fencer is to find room under his opponent's arm . . .

. . . and to make the blade bend laterally rather than perpendicularly, thus avoiding the possibility or coming in contact with his opponent's arm.

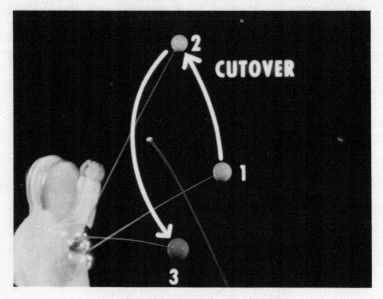

Another attack, the cutover, is similar to the disengagement. This, instead of passing under the blade, passes over the opponent's blade to end in the opposite side or position to that of the engagement.

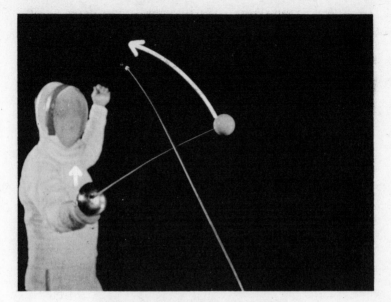

In the cutover, the weapon arm is drawn back slightly, at the same time the forearm is raised partially, with a slight bending of the wrist. The fencer's blade should slip over the opponent's blade until it has cleared it by passing over the point.

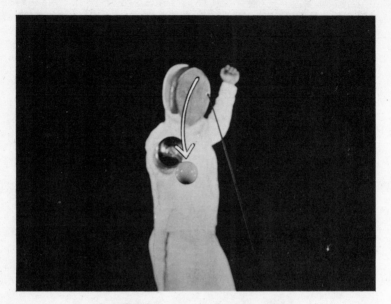

Immediately upon clearing the adversary's point, the forearm should be brought down and forward smartly to a threatening and extended position with the point in line, and on the other side of his blade.

Besides these deceptive attacks, which
involved no actions against the blade,
there are such offensive movements which
pave the way for the final attack.

BEAT

The beat shown is one of the several aggressive actions that can be made
against an opponent's blade.

The beat is a crisp, sudden and precise movement of one blade made against the other to knock it aside or to obtain a reaction. By quickly opening and closing the last three fingers of the hand, the fencer can detach his blade from his opponent's and bring it back smartly, thus knocking it aside.

BEAT-LUNGE

The beat combined with a lunge is another direct attack!

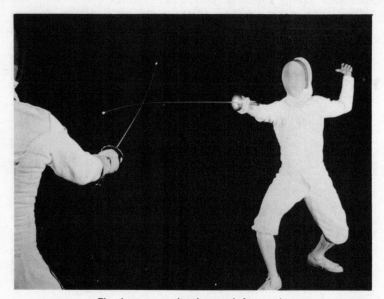

The beat can also be used for an indirect attack. For example, beat . . .

. . . disengage—lunge . . . and score!

PRESSURE

A pressure on the blade can also be used as a preparatory action. It involves a more pronounced and prolonged action on the blade than the beat. It is a pressure of one blade upon another in order to deflect it or to obtain a reaction from it. This is achieved with a combination of the contraction of the last three fingers of the hand and a slight flexing of the wrist.

PRESSURE-LUNGE

Pressure followed by the lunge is another direct attack.

The completed attack is one of continuous movement. All direct attacks must be executed in a single forward flowing, driving movement. Here is a reprise demonstrated by a young Olympian performer. Maintaining a high level of performance or learning to become a proficient fencer depends largely on daily practice in the fundamentals of foil fencing.

3

ELEMENTARY DEFENSE

Footwork is the foundation of the fencer.
Body control and mobility with proper
footwork can only be acquired through
constant practice.

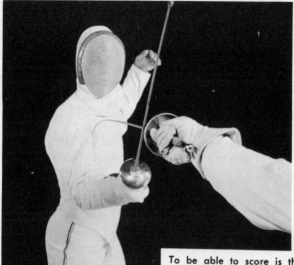

To be able to score is the goal of all fencers. As a result a great deal of practice should be devoted to the attack. But, the fencer should also be concerned with learning how to avoid being hit.

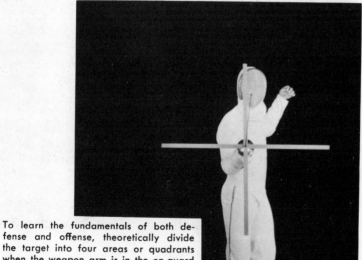

To learn the fundamentals of both defense and offense, theoretically divide the target into four areas or quadrants when the weapon arm is in the on-guard position.

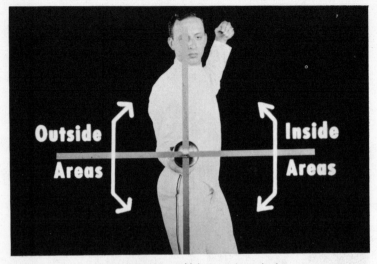

The vertical line which runs through the bell of the weapon divides the target into two sections, called outside areas and inside areas.

The horizontal line which runs through the bell of the weapon divides the target into two sections, called highline areas and lowline areas.

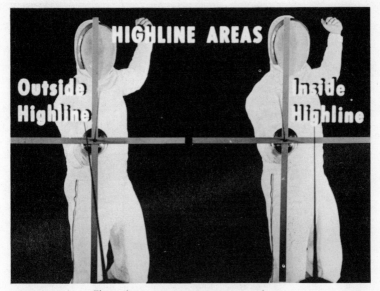

Thus, there are two areas or quadrants
above the horizontal line, and . . .

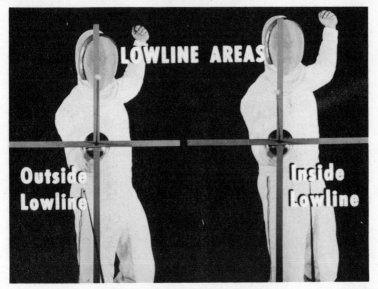

. . . there are two areas or quadrants
below the horizontal line.

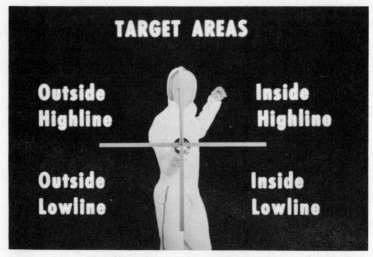

TARGET AREAS

Outside Highline

Inside Highline

Outside Lowline

Inside Lowline

Therefore, the complete target area is now divided into four quadrants: Outside highline area, inside highline area, outside lowline area, and inside lowline area.

To defend the target areas, a fencer must learn to parry or block the opponent's weapon with his blade. However, before learning to parry or block . . .

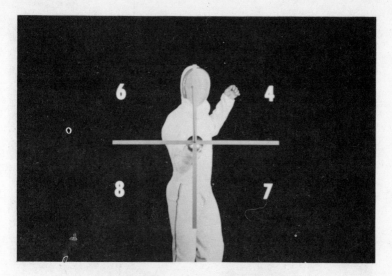

. . . you must understand that although there are *two* theoretical fencing positions corresponding to each area or quadrant, only sixth, fourth, eighth and seventh, which are numerically classified as shown, are the fundamental or the basic defensive positions which will be studied in the following sequences.

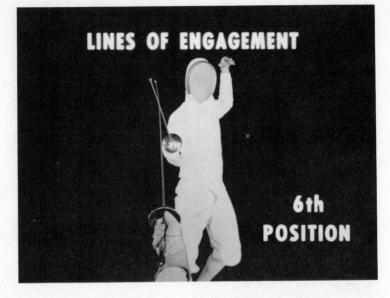

LINES OF ENGAGEMENT

6th
POSITION

(Above) A fencing position is the position which is assumed by two fencers when their blades are crossed or engaged. Here two fencers have engaged blades in the sixth position whereby the high outside lines are closed to each of them. Fencing positions and fencing lines are practically synonymous.

(Opposite page, above) The fencer, when in sixth position, will obscure all target area in the high outside line quadrant to his opponent.

(Opposite page, below) The correct hand position for sixth for right-handed fencers, as seen from above, shows the fingers at twelve o'clock and the thumb at two o'clock position—palm up, pommel alongside wrist, blade angulated upward above bell, with point at eye level at about the one o'clock position.

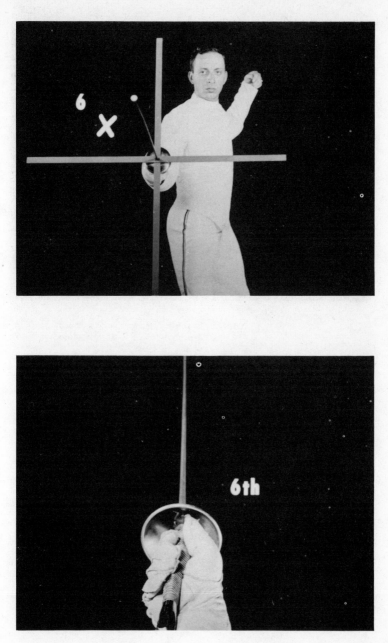

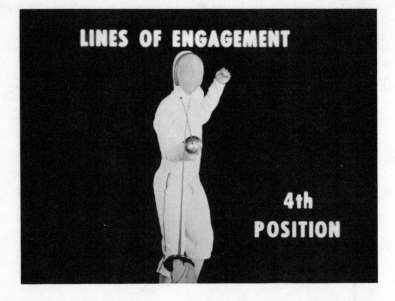

LINES OF ENGAGEMENT

4th
POSITION

(Above) Engaging blades in the fourth position, the high inside lines are closed to each of the fencers.

(Opposite page, above) The fencer, when in fourth position, will obscure all target area in the high inside line quadrant to his opponent.

(Opposite page, below) The correct hand position for fourth for right-handed fencers, as seen from above, shows the thumb at twelve o'clock and fingers and palm at nine o'clock position. Wrist is flexed, and the pommel moves away from the wrist, blade is angulated upward above bell, with point at eye level and at about twelve o'clock position.

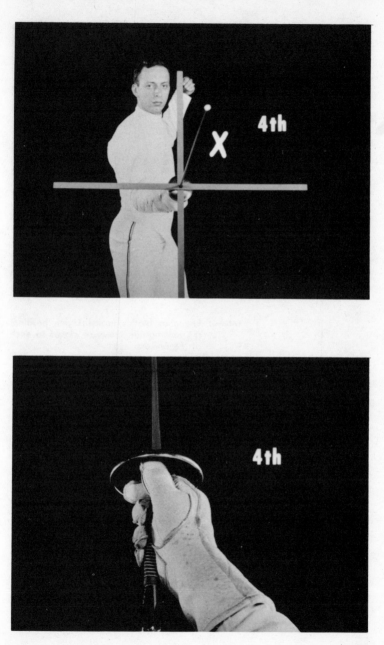

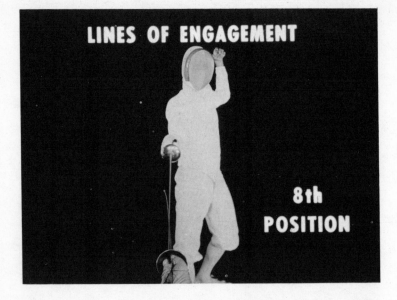

LINES OF ENGAGEMENT

8th POSITION

(Above)   Engaging blades in the eighth position, the low outside lines are closed to each of the fencers.

(Opposite page, above)   The fencer, when in the eighth position, as illustrated, will obscure all target area in the low outside line quadrant to his opponent.

(Opposite page, below)   The correct hand position for eighth for right-handed fencers, as seen from above, shows the fingers at twelve o'clock and the thumb at two o'clock position—palm up, pommel slightly off the wrist, blade is angulated below bell level, with point at about five o'clock position.

8th X

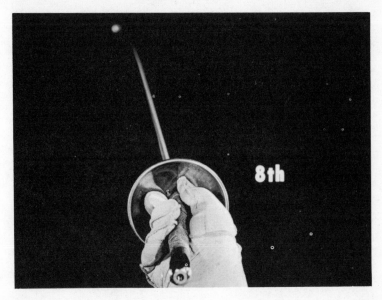

8th

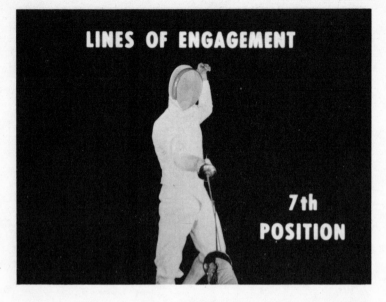

LINES OF ENGAGEMENT

7th
POSITION

(Above) Engaging blades in the seventh position, the low inside lines are closed to each of the fencers.

(Opposite page, above) The fencer, when in the seventh position, as shown, will obscure all the target area in the low inside line quadrant to his opponent.

(Opposite page, below) The correct hand position for seventh for right-handed fencers, as seen from above, shows the fingers and palm at twelve o'clock and the thumb at two o'clock position. Wrist is flexed, and pommel is off and above the wrist, blade is angulated below bell level, with point at about seven o'clock position.

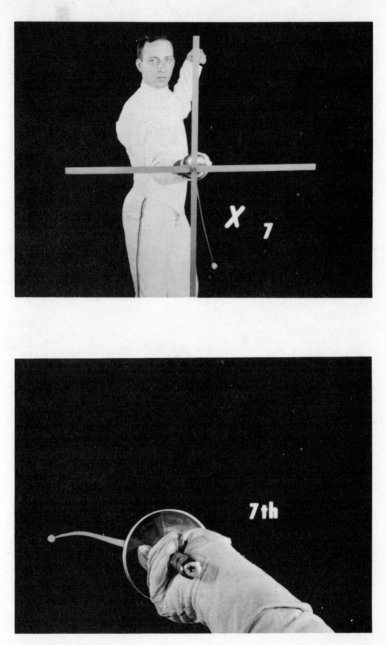

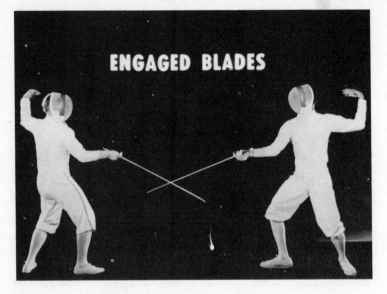

ENGAGED BLADES

Therefore, when you cross blades with
your opponent . . .

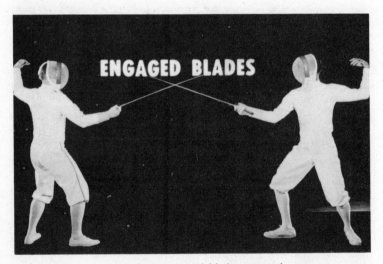

ENGAGED BLADES

. . . you have engaged blades or are in
a state of engagement.

COVERING

To be covered or to have the target area closed to your opponent is to engage blades . . .

. . . in such a way that the area in which the blades are crossed is closed to a direct thrust or attack.

In the bout, the fencer on the right is covering or protecting his high outside line area from a direct attack by engaging in sixth. However, his inside line areas, as well as his opponent's are vulnerable to an attack.

CHANGE OF
ENGAGEMENT

The fencer, therefore, executes a rapid
change of engagement to the high inside
line area by passing the blade under-
neath his opponent's and then engaging
him in the fourth position.

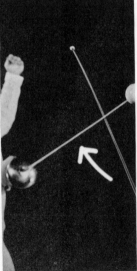

To change his engagement from sixth, by means of fingerplay, the fencer drops his point and passes it under his opponent's blade. Then, he lifts it up again and engages blades in fourth—the new line of engagement.

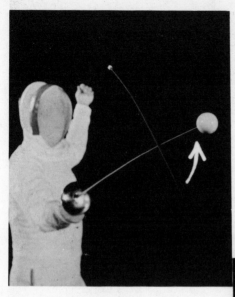

This process of changing engagements can be reversed. To change his engagement from fourth, by means of finger-play he drops his point and passes it under his opponent's blade. Then he lifts it up again and engages blades in sixth—the new line of engagement.

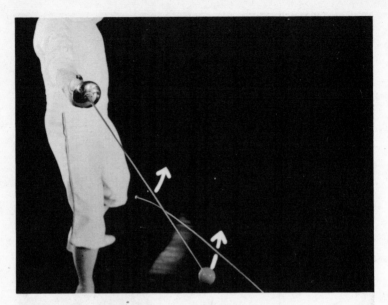

When blades are engaged in eighth, as
illustrated, or seventh positions, the
change of engagement is executed by
lifting the blade *over* the opponent's and
engaging his blade in the opposite line.
There must be no change in the elevation
of the weapon-arm when executing *any*
change of engagement.

Since changes of engagement can be deceived, its execution must be swiftly and precisely made and quickly terminated. As the fencer on the right advances, while changing his engagement . . .

. . . his opponent anticipating his move has taken advantage of the loss of distance and scores easily while his opponent is off balance.

ABSENCE OF BLADE

Constant actions or changes of engagements on the blade by a strong or
heavy-handed opponent will tend to tire
the weapon-arm. Therefore, it might be
to a fencers advantage to *avoid engaging* blades.

To have any value, this action must be
premeditated and deliberate because
with absence of blade, both fencers'
target areas are open. A fencer must
know how to maneuver his weapon to
avoid any attempt by his opponent to
regain blade contact, or in an attempt to
score.

The principle of defense or parrying for the defender is to learn to properly angulate his foil where he brings his blade's strong area, called the forte, against the attacking blade's weak section, called the foible.

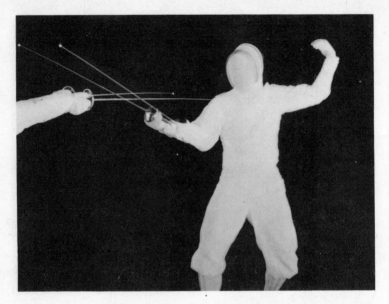

Defense consists of a variety of movements or parries used to ward off or
block offensive actions.

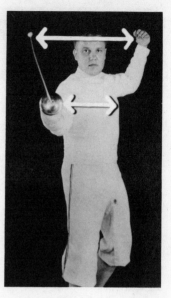

Lateral parries are controlled movements made by the defender.

The defender carries his weapon-arm and his foil across his body in a horizontal plane.

91

PARRY 4th

When in sixth position and threatened by an attack in fourth, carry the foil from the outside to the inside sufficiently to close the area being attacked. This is called parry fourth.

PARRY 6th

When in fourth position and threatened by an attack in sixth, carry the foil from the inside to the outside sufficiently to close the area being attacked. This is called parry sixth.

Semicircular parries are those which move from a highline engagement to block or deflect an attack directed into the lowline area, or from a lowline engagement to a highline position.

The blade describes a half circle when moving from high to low or low to high.

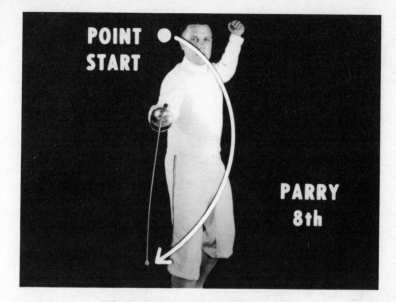

When engaged in sixth and threatened in the lowline area, the defender's blade should describe a half circle ending in the eighth position. This is called parry eighth.

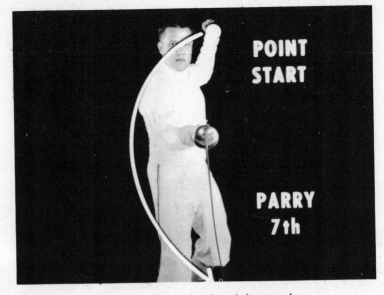

POINT
START

PARRY
7th

When engaged in fourth and threatened
in the lowline area, the defender's blade
should describe a half circle moving into
seventh position. This is called parry
seventh.

The circular or counter-parries are those which, by describing a circular movement of the blade . . .

. . . bring the attacker's blade back to the line from which it started.

PARRY COUNTER 6th

When engaged in sixth and threatened
by a disengagement attack, the defender
describes a circular movement of the
blade, gathers in the aggressor's blade
and brings it back into the line of sixth.
This is called parry counter-sixth.

PARRY COUNTER 4th

When engaged in fourth and threatened by a disengagement attack, the defender describes a circular movement of the blade, gathers in the aggressor's blade and brings it back into the line of fourth. This is called parry counter-fourth.

The importance of defense cannot be overemphasized. A fencer cannot win without knowing how to defend himself and can hardly lose when possessing a perfect defense. From the defensive position, the fencer on the right . . .

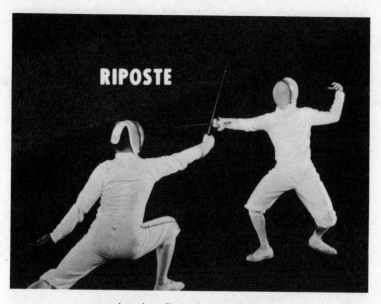

RIPOSTE

... takes the offense by scoring with a riposte. A riposte is a counter-offensive action executed after a successful parry. A riposte can employ *any* of the attacks as a counter movement. A fencer to win—must score!

4

STRATEGY AND TACTICS

Once you have mastered the fundamentals of fencing, competition is awaiting you!

There is an exciting and exhilarating feeling when crossing blades with an opponent. Fencing is an exchange of personalities, strategies, and actions at almost unbelievable speed. The fencers in combat are free individuals, dependent solely upon themselves. It is personal combat at its finest!

Fencing has no physical limitations. Anyone can fence. But a thorough knowledge of the fundamentals is a necessity. You must study and constantly practice these fundamentals to attain a high degree of proficiency in their execution. To attain success in competition, however, requires more than just a sound technique.

Another essential requirement is to be able to *plan the proper action* which will score against the opponent's style, technique and tactics. You only need to know *when, how,* and *where* to thrust your blade.

Attack, for example, while your opponent
is *in the process* of covering up one line,
by entering into his opening line!

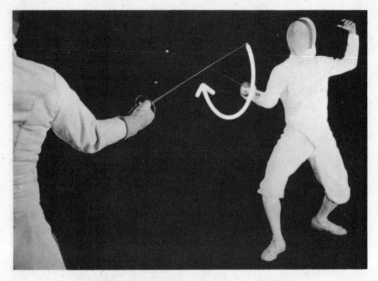

When deceiving your opponent's blade, offensive blade actions are usually made up of semicircular or circular movements.

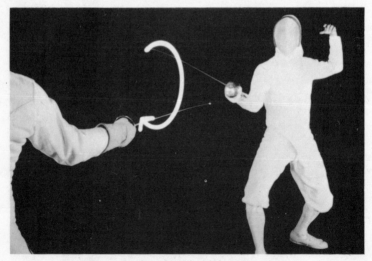

For example, when the defense is using a circular or counter-parry . . .

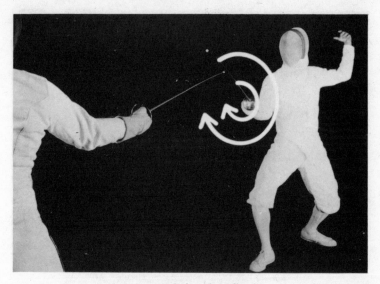

...it is essential that the offensive actions move in the same direction.

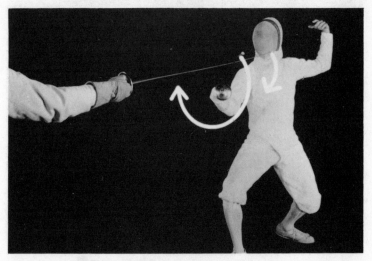

This principle permits an attacker to employ an action known as...

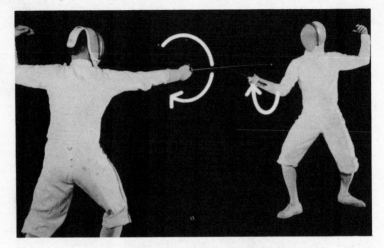

The Double! The fencer extends his weapon-arm with a disengage, his opponent starts to execute a circular or counter-parry to bring the aggressor's blade back to his closed line, but...

...the attacker deceives this attempt by following him around and lunges into his open line and scores!

An opponent's reactions can be found by different means, but the obvious method is to execute simple attacks, which he will have to parry . . .

. . . wait for his riposte, which will be deflected, . . .

...and carefully select the target-area for the counterattack!

It is possible to anticipate the adversary's defense through observation.

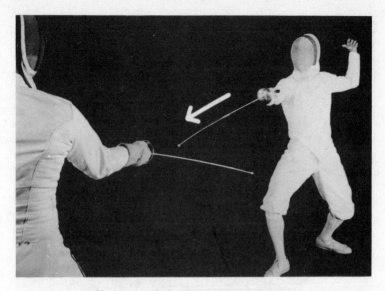

Having noted the opponent's reaction to a feint . . .

. . . or his preference for certain parries, the attacker has a much better chance of *anticipating* and deceiving them.

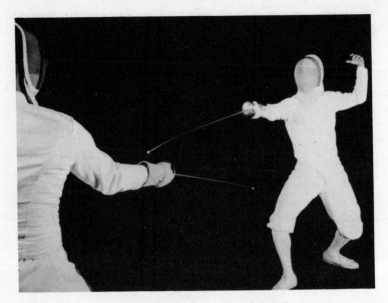

With this knowledge of his opponent's
defense the attacking fencer will be
better able to deceive his opponent's
blade and quickly score.

Speed, though, is a quality which can be a handicap as well as an asset! A clever fencer will regulate his speed carefully to fit in or time with his opponent's speed of reaction. This regulation of speed is known as cadence or rhythm. Fencers of experience often change their cadence and effectively hinder the opponent in his efforts to regulate his. This change of speed often catches the opponent by surprise and places him off-balance. While off-balance a fencer can be readily hit!

STOP-HIT

Change in tactics, such as employing a
Stop-Thrust or Time-Thrust, can also surprise a fencer, and a hit can be scored
before he can regain his balance and
change his tactics.

STOP-HIT

A stop-hit is a counter-offensive movement which stops and hits a fencer while
he is developing his attack.

FLECHE ATTACK

Here is a fencer scoring with a stop-hit against a fleche or running attack.

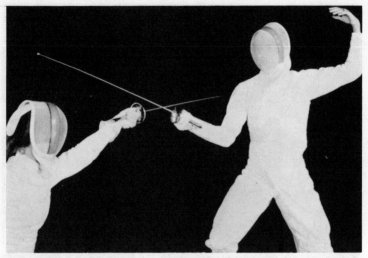

Occasionally a right-handed fencer will find a left-hander opposing him. This will present certain difficulties.

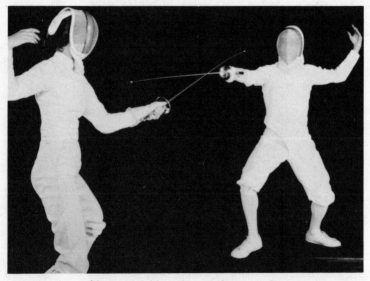

It's not surprising, since performance, instruction and practice have primarily been against other right-handed fencers and teachers.

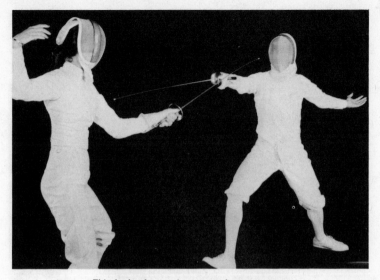

This lack of experience can be overcome in two ways: First, the right-handed fencer should fence left-handed opponents as often as possible.

Second, your coach or teacher should use his left hand occasionally while giving lessons.

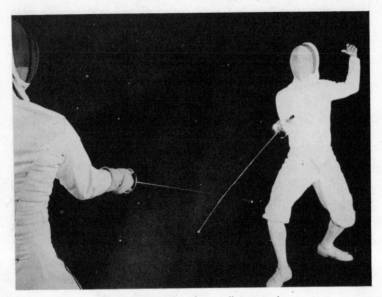

In retrospect, therefore, all aggressive *arm* actions, no matter how simple or complex they become, stem from three fundamentals . . .

THE
BEAT

. . . the beat or an action on the blade . . .

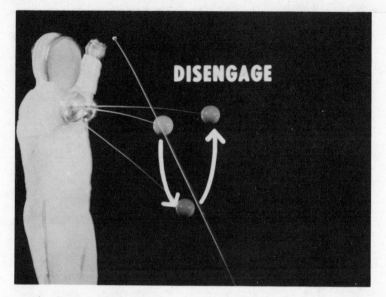

... the disengagement ...

... and the thrust.

Expert coaching and instruction will be necessary to develop variations and progression from these fundamentals.

However, final strategy and tactics will vary with individual fencers and with individual styles. The decision to attack must be made before any physical action is taken. The attack itself should be but a conditioned reflex.

Success in fencing, therefore, depends on the fencer's ability to select and use the correct tactics with precision, coordination and timing which will score against his opponent's particular style and game!

GLOSSARY OF TERMS

A.F.L.A.—Amateur Fencers League of America.

ABSENCE OF BLADE—When the weapons are not in contact.

ADVANCE—Forward movement of the feet with the leading foot stepping out first and then followed by an equal displacement of the trailing foot without crossing them as in walking or running.

AIDS—The last three fingers of the weapon-hand.

ATTACK—Usually the initial action of a phrase or sequence of play. It consists of a forward movement of the weapon threatening the opponent's valid target.

ATTACK ON PREPARATION—It is executed just as the opponent is about to start his own attack, but before the opponent's attack has actually begun.

ATTACK ON THE BLADE—A preparation of attack by beat, pressure or froissement.

BALESTRA—A method of advancing with a quick jump forward.

BARRAGE—Fence-off between two or more fencers for a qualifying position.

BEAT—A preparation of attack.

BIND—A preparation of attack which carries the opponent's blade diagonally across from a highline to a lowline area, or vice versa.

BREAKING GROUND—Retreating or stepping back out of distance with both feet.

BROKEN TIME—When two movements are deliberately not made to follow immediately upon one another.

CADENCE—Rhythm in which a sequence of movements is made.

CEDE—Partially to give way to an opposition.

CENTRAL GUARD—A position of the hand between the two lateral lines, i.e., between fourth and sixth.

CHANGE OF ENGAGEMENT—The action of engaging in a new line.

CLOSE QUARTERS—When two fencers are close together, but can still wield their weapons effectively.

COMPOUND ATTACKS—Attacks composed of one or more feints.

COMPOUND PRISES DE FER—An uninterrupted succession of takings of the blade.

COMPOUND RIPOSTES—Ripostes composed of one or more feints.

CORPS-A-CORPS—Body to body or more familiarly called a clinch.

COULE—A preparation of attack by pressure; a glide of one's blade along the opponent's.

COUNTER-DISENGAGEMENT—A simple offensive action deceiving a change of engagement or a counter-parry.

COUNTER-OFFENSIVE ACTIONS—The stop-hit and the time-hit.

COUNTER-PARRY—A parry describing a circle.

COUNTER-RIPOSTE—The offensive action which follows the successful parry of a riposte.

COUNTER-TIME—A movement of second intention.

COUPE—Cut-over.

COVERED—A position which closes the line of engagement.

CROISE—A taking of the blade which carries the opponent's blade from highline area to lowline area on the same side as the engagement, but does not, as in the bind, carry it diagonally across.

CUT-OVER—A form of disengagement which passes over the blade.

CUTTING THE LINES—Describing circular parries made other than in the line of engagement.

DELAYED—Generally refers to a riposte which is not executed immediately following the parry.

DEROBEMENT—Blade movements executed with an extended arm which evade the opponent's attempts to beat or take the blade.

DETACHMENT—A parry, which by its crispness leaves the blade immediately after it has met it.

DEVELOPMENT—The combined actions of the extension of the weapon-arm and the lunge.

DIRECT—Term denoting that an attack or a riposte has been delivered in the line of engagement.

DISENGAGEMENT—A simple attack, or riposte, which consists of leaving the line of engagement to go into the opposite one—known also as a disengage.

DOUBLE—An attack deceiving a counter-parry.

DOUBLE PRISE DE FER—A succession of takings of the blade where contact is lost between each one.

DOUBLE TOUCH—This is an official's decision which means that the entire action is annulled, and that the fencers are to be put back on guard without a score for either.

ENGAGEMENT—The crossing of the weapons and the contact made thereby.

ENVELOPMENT—A taking of the blade which, by describing a circle with both blades in contact, returns to the line of engagement.

F.I.E.—Federation Internationale d'Escrime.

FALSE ATTACK—An attack which is not intended to land.

FEINT—A movement of the blade meant to resemble an attack and whose purpose is to draw a reaction.

FENCING MEASURE—The practical distance between two fencers.

FENCING POSITIONS—The classical positions in which the weapon-arm and the weapon may be placed.

FIELD OF PLAY—The arena which includes the piste and its extensions, strip or mat.

FINGER PLAY—A method of manipulating the weapon with the fingers.

FIRST COUNTER-RIPOSTE—The attacker's first riposte.

FLECHE—A running attack, i.e., an action of the legs permitting the fencer to reach his opponent by running instead of lunging.

FOIBLE—The half of the blade nearest the point.

FOIL—Originally the practice weapon. In modern fencing has become a basic and competitive weapon.

FORTE—The half of the blade nearest the guard or bell.

FROISSEMENT—A preparation of attack by grazing the opponent's blade very strongly and sharply, thus deflecting it.

GAINING GROUND—Advancing or stepping forward with both feet.

GRIP—The manner in which the weapon is held.

GUARD—A piece of metal for the protection of the fingers, which is inserted between the blade and the handle. Sometimes called the bell.

HIT—Touch or score on valid target with point of weapon which stimulates a "puncture-type" wound.

IMMEDIATE—Generally refers to a riposte which follows a parry without a pause.

INDIRECT—Any single offensive action into the opposite side or area from the original position of the blades.

JUDGES—Those whose duty it is to watch for hits and assist the president.

JURY—Composed of a president and four judges.

LINES—Theoretical areas corresponding to the fencing positions.

LUNGE—Fundamental movement in the attack used to reach the opponent's target. It is a forward movement of the body executed by advancing the leading foot in the direction of the opponent, while the trailing foot remains stationary.

MANIPULATORS—The index finger (forefinger) and thumb of the hand holding the weapon.

N.C.A.A.—National Collegiate Athletic Association.

N.F.C.A.A.—National Fencing Coaches Association of America.

ON GUARD—The position of feet, body, and arms, adopted by the fencer preparatory to actions of offensive or defensive nature.

ONE-TWO—Two disengagements which end in the original line.

PARRY—Defensive action executed with the blade or guard or both that blocks, deviates, or deflects the opponent's offensive action from scoring.

PHRASE or PHRASE D'ARMES—Period of continuous action without any cessation by both fencers. The phrase is ended when the continuous sequence is interrupted, even if only for a brief moment.

PISTE—A limited area within which the fencers compete, i.e., strip or mat.

POMMEL—A conical piece of metal which serves the dual purpose of locking the different parts of the weapon and acting as a counter-weight to the blade.

POOL—Tournament term where several fencers are assigned to compete against each other, i.e., preliminary pool or round, semi-final pool or round.

PREPARATION OF ATTACK—A blade, body, or foot movement which opens the way for the attack.

PRESIDENT—The umpire in fencing, previously known as the Director.

PRESSURE—A preparation of attack made by pressing upon the opponent's blade.

PRINCIPLE OF DEFENSE—The opposition of forte to foible, or proper angulation of blade.

PROGRESSIVE ATTACKS—A method of executing certain compound attacks.

RECOVERY OR RETURN TO ON-GUARD—The action of returning from the development, i.e., returning to the on-guard.

REDOUBLEMENT—A renewal of attack, while in the lunge, comprising one or more blade movements.

REMISE—A renewal of attack, while in the lunge, made by replacing the point on the target in the line of the parry.

REPRISE—A renewal of attack preceded by a forward return to the on-guard position.

RETREAT—Backward movement of the feet with the trailing foot stepping out first and then followed by an equal displacement of the leading foot without crossing them as in walking or running.

RIPOSTE—The offensive action which follows a successful parry.

SECOND COUNTER-RIPOSTE—The defender's second riposte.

SECOND INTENTION—This is a false attack, which the attacker intends shall be parried by the defender, in the expectation that the attacker may then parry the defender's riposte and score on the counter-riposte.

SEMICIRCULAR PARRY—A parry describing a half-circle from the highline area to the lowline area, or vice versa.

SIMPLE ATTACK—One which is direct or indirect.

SIMPLE PARRY—Direct movement of the blade in a horizontal or lateral plane to meet the attacker's blade and deflect or block it from scoring.

STANCE—The position of the feet and part of the on-guard position.

STOP-HIT—A counter-offensive action which, to be valid, must land before the attacker's final movement.

STRAIGHT THRUST—A direct and simplest form of attack.

STRIP—Piste, field of play or area, or mat upon which fencers compete.

SUCCESSIVE PARRIES—Several parries following one upon the other until the attacking blade is found.

TAKING OF THE BLADE—A preparation of attack.

TIME-HIT—A counter-offensive action which anticipates and intercepts the final line of the attack, blocking it from scoring.

TO TIME—To seize an opportunity and to execute a stroke at the correct moment.

TROMPEMENT—Offensive blade actions which deceive the opponent's parries.

UNCOVERED—A position where the line of engagement is not closed.

WARNING LINES—Lines drawn one meter from the rear limits of the strip or piste at which fencers are warned that they are nearing the end lines of the mat or fencing area.

INDEX